T0128035

CONVERSATIONS
with RALPH

A series of conversations with a humble
Intergalactic Being about the mysteries of the Universe.

MICHELLE LIGHTWORKER

BALBOA.
PRESS
A DIVISION OF HAY HOUSE

Copyright © 2018 Michelle Lightworker.

All rights reserved. No part of this book may be used or reproduced by
any means, graphic, electronic, or mechanical, including photocopying,
recording, taping or by any information storage retrieval system
without the written permission of the author except in the case of
brief quotations embodied in critical articles and reviews.

John 1:1 New International Version

Balboa Press books may be ordered through booksellers or by contacting:

Balboa Press
A Division of Hay House
1663 Liberty Drive
Bloomington, IN 47403
www.balboapress.com.au
1 (877) 407-4847

Because of the dynamic nature of the Internet, any web addresses or
links contained in this book may have changed since publication and
may no longer be valid. The views expressed in this work are solely those
of the author and do not necessarily reflect the views of the publisher,
and the publisher hereby disclaims any responsibility for them.

The author of this book does not dispense medical advice or prescribe the use
of any technique as a form of treatment for physical, emotional, or medical
problems without the advice of a physician, either directly or indirectly. The
intent of the author is only to offer information of a general nature to help you
in your quest for emotional and spiritual well-being. In the event you use any
of the information in this book for yourself, which is your constitutional right,
the author and the publisher assume no responsibility for your actions.

Any people depicted in stock imagery provided by Getty Images are
models, and such images are being used for illustrative purposes only.
Certain stock imagery © Getty Images.

Print information available on the last page.

ISBN: 978-1-5043-1435-0 (sc)
ISBN: 978-1-5043-1437-4 (e)

Balboa Press rev. date: 08/16/2018

CHAPTER 1

The Flower of Life Phenomena

10 April 2018 — My 'Pre-Conversation' experience

Since 2009 whenever I closed my eyes I would see the Flower of Life Mandala. It was never static, always spinning gently.

I originally awoke and noticed it as I lay in my bed with my eyes closed. Then it kept appearing each morning. I didn't really know what to do about it or why it was there. Something inside me told me that it was there to teach me. So I decided to experiment with it. I meditated on it and asked specific questions or focused on a person. Then I noticed almost immediately a colour would appear. With it, a message. The energy would flow up or down, signifying a lighter or heavier vibration. Different colours would symbolise where a person's energy was blocked in relation to their chakras. Information would come out of it in shapes too when I asked each question. The colour, shape and directional flow of energy would repeat until I understood the message behind it. Then I would get even more information.

The Flower of Life phenomenon was only there when I wanted to focus on it. It never got in my way or tried to divert my attention to it. I thought it was just an information portal of sorts. However, 9 years later, it was very different. I was about to embark on an unexpected journey only spanning a short time, which was to provide answers to life's greatest mysteries.

Before we go there, let's take quick moment to see how the Flower of Life is perceived. This is what it looks like:

The Flower of Life

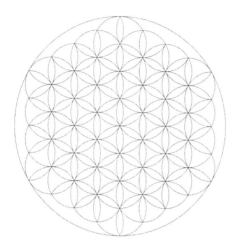

The Flower of Life is a very interesting geometric shape. It is only comprised of circles that overlap each other in an evenly spaced fashion. The end result is that it looks like a flower! It has been known over history to inspire philosophers, architects and artists all over the world. And it was only upon putting this book together that I learned that it had held religious value depicting the fundamental forms of space and time. I also discovered that it is known to contain a type of Akashic Record of basic information of all living things. This Flower of Life is seen as the visual expression of the connections of life that run through all sentient beings. I couldn't believe it when I also discovered that there are groups of people all over the world who meditate on the Flower of Life. This was certain validation of this journey I was embarking on.

And 4dshift.com describes; "We see the Flower of Life present instantly when life begins in the world as the embryo begins to take shape. See the embryonic progression in the diagram below:

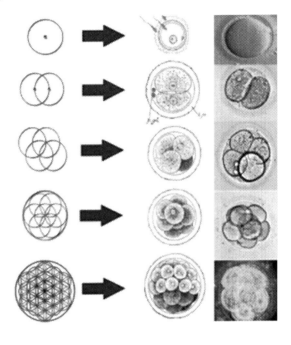

Early pioneers in our modern world: Buckminster Fuller, Rudolph Steiner, Richard Lawlor and Drunvalo Melchizdek spent decades recovering this ancient knowledge. Many researchers have joined them. Frank Chester is now leading the research in the discovery of new sacred forms contained with the Flower of Life that now reveal the sacred geometry of organic forms where the geometry was unexplained."

I was no stranger to the power of this incredible 'Being' however I had no idea what it was truly capable of. Up until then, I had no real motivation or inclination to explore it. I knew from studying the Orientation in Anthroposophy back in 1994 that the Flower of Life was taught in Rudolf Steiner's Waldorf Eduction as the basis of all geometric shapes. So I knew it was special. How could a diagram encompassing the basis of all human life and shapes not be special? But what I wasn't expecting was that it chose to reveal itself, without me seeking. I am always of the mind that we have free will. Free will allows us to explore our expansion as a human and spiritual being. However, free will is also contained in preparation and readiness. I was obviously ready and prepared for what was next to come.

On this particular morning in April of 2018, I saw it spinning but it was drawing forward, like a tunnel. It had never done this before. It was magnetic and drawing me forward too. I noticed it got smaller and smaller and I felt like I wanted to follow it. I noticed that it was indeed a tunnel that I was walking through. Even though I was not moving on the bed I was meditating on, I still felt as if it was real. I was lucid. I was lucid astral travelling but with such a clear physical sensation that I felt I was bi-locating. Bilocation is the ability to be in 2 places at once.

Within a very short amount of time, I came to the end of this tunnel. At the end of the tunnel, I saw crystalline structures, right at the edge. I knew at that moment, I was not only in outer space, I was in a completely different universe. Not a parallel universe. A completely different universe.

Then as quickly as I arrived and had that realisation, I was back. Woah! What was that? Where did that come from? It felt so random.

Then I saw the spinning flower of life again and I was again led into it. This time, the tunnel was more organic. I put out my hand to feel it. Once again, even though I had not moved an inch in my bed, I could definitely feel the sides of the tunnel. It felt organic, like soft spongy moss. And I noticed that there was a kind of plant growing and swaying on the sides of the tunnel. Almost like sea anemone but I instinctively knew I was definitely not under water. At the end of each tunnel, I was again at the precipice of a new Universe. Another new Universe? Two new Universe visits in one morning? This was blowing my mind.

Up until then, I had thought there was only one Universe. In fact, I hadn't really thought about it at all. I can only assume that I thought there was only 1 universe up until that point.

I saw a flying squid like animal. But I reiterate that I knew I was definitely not underwater. It was vast expanse. I saw many stars and planets. I had the instant realisation that physical life did not abide by the laws of physics of our earthly World. Or should I say "Universe". I knew I had just visited 2 separate locations of 2 very different Universes.

I thought that this was enough information to process for a while. Little did I knew what was about to happen just 4 days later....

CHAPTER 2

Everything is Seen

14 April 2018 — Conversation 1

This morning I awoke and unexpectedly saw the spinning flower of life again. I felt it drawing me forward. Another adventure? I followed its magnetic pull. As I travelled along – or as it continued before me - I noticed purple flashes of light on the sides of the tunnel. Once I reached the end of the tunnel, I expected to experience what I had previously in the 4 days prior. I expected to arrive at the end of the tunnel and stand at the precipice of a new Universe. Or was it one of the previous ones? I was not sure. But for some reason I saw the flowing purple light before me and I asked, "Where am I?" Then I was shown that the purple light WAS in fact the end of the tunnel. I WAS out the other side. I was in a new Universe. And I knew it was a new Universe in that moment. I hadn't had a sensation of flying so I hadn't realised I had passed through the end. And so then I realised I was looking at the end of the tunnel from beyond it. Looking back, as it were. And so, then I realised that I was actually IN this new universe. The purple colour was significant in the resonance of this universe and I was about to find out why.

For the first time, I was in another Universe consciously. I turned around of course expecting to see stars, however I did not. I did not see planets. I wondered, "Where are they?". I saw a whole heap of what looked like Spiritual beings like droplets of ink in water. A variety of colours. The occasional face, like a torch was lighting up a part of it. No body, just face. This didn't make any sense at the time, but there was a big reason why, which I later discovered.

And then not really knowing what to do next, I asked the question, "What is the highest vibration here?" I heard a response, "Peace". I immediately felt that this was a safe place to be. I was then curious as to finding out what the lowest vibration was in this new universe. "Depression" was the answer. I was shown this in the form of a downward flow of energy into a dark void. I did not understand why depression was the lowest vibration that existed here, but I soon found out how important it was and why.

Then I noticed a Being before me – it had no body, face or colour, but I knew it was there. I later found out his name was Ralph and we formally introduced ourselves, but this was not my first experience at all. My first experience with Ralph was him commencing telling me all about the Universe I was in. And it became a back and forth conversation that flowed effortlessly. I can only summarise here what was discussed as I did not capture the order of things transpiring. It was completely unexpected. However, as I write this, I endeavour to capture future conversations real time whether by a voice recording or typing, I know not which at this point, but I will go in prepared. As I know after this first conversation, I have many questions.

I learned that I was in a Universe full of contradictions, which I plan to explain. Beings here were human but did not look human at all. This universe had no physical existence, yet it was not a place 'beyond' life. There was no place to go yet all could be found right here before one left. There was nothing to see, yet everything was capable of being seen at all times.

I debriefed with my husband straight after my experience. As you can imagine I was still half asleep. I decided to record our discussion and capture any questions that arose. This was a really good idea. I had questions and I knew he would too. And he did...

Me: Just had this experience and I woke up and I saw the Flower of Life and it was pulling me forward again, not pulling, but I could tell it was calling me to go down, so I was like, "Okay". It was really different this time. It had purple flashes and stuff along the way. And I got to the end of it and I didn't know I was out the other side. Because I was seeing a lot of almost like flying spirits of different sorts and the occasional face and it was almost like a torch was shined on the face. It was weird. It was like all different kinds of spirits everywhere and all things everywhere flying. You know if you put a piece of dye in water, that's how they looked. And I was like, ok and I basically asked the question, "What's the highest vibration here?". I got shown that as I came out the other side, I was looking back towards the tunnel. So I was there but I didn't know I'd gone through because you don't have that sensation of flying. You're there but you don't know you're moving. You know what I mean? So, it was hard for me to realise I was on the other side. I had to be told that I am on the other side. Then I was shown that that I had gone through. Then I asked, well I didn't know what to do really, and I just sort of said, "What's the highest vibration here?" and I got "Peace". That's what I was told. And then I said, "Okay well what's the lowest vibration here?" and I got "Depression". And I was like, "really depression?". And then I realised there was a 'Being' in front of me. And I started talking to them and I found out that their name was Ralph and they were helping me to understand their universe.

I was told that this was not a parallel Universe, it was its own thing. I was told this very clearly. I was told that that they had evolved past each incarnation that they had, and this was their last incarnation and this was like they were still spirits. It was not like they had died. It's kind of hard to explain. It's really important to get this bit. He said, "It's not like everybody just died and we're all just here experiencing our last incarnation, it was more we have lived through the human experience". A lot of them had experienced what we had experienced, like experiencing the Christ coming, even though it was not a parallel universe. They had created and done similar things we'd done because it was part of the human process and part of the human evolution of consciousness. They had now gotten to this point where they didn't have the physical anymore. So, it wasn't like there were planets and stuff. It was just them. He said, "You might find this really difficult to understand but we are not dead, we are still alive". And I said, "Yes, this is really difficult to understand". And he said, "We've evolved past the body, but we haven't quite transitioned to the other side completely not needing to have this experience. We are still souls". They have definite personalities. He said, "You would think that not having a body would be easier but it's often harder". What they have access to, which was really interesting, was that they can have a conversation with me and they can see every single past life I've ever had. And they do that with each other too when they're having a conversation. Their whole point of being in this last incarnation is to process anything that's holding them back from that last final stage. While they're having these conversations with each other; although they can't see anything and they can't do anything and they can't go anywhere and they don't have a purpose and they don't have any of that stuff like driving them, right, they're whole sole purpose is to…

Hubby: What about time, are they conscious of time?

Me: I haven't gotten to that part yet. But I'll just finish what I'm talking about and maybe you can tell me. But what they do have access to…I would say yes, I'm getting a yes on that by the way. Yes, there is time but it is not like they're governed by the clock, but it is a process of time. If you were gonna measure someone from where they are, to where they've got to go, - not that someone else is measuring it - in our sense it is taking time. Because he did mention to me it is a process. And he said to me, what he was trying to teach me was the 'process of their process'. That's what he said, the words "Process of their process". And he explained the depression thing, because he said, "When you have no purpose when you have no 'thing' when you have no….", you know what I mean? When you have no family…

Hubby: No sensation…

Me: No sensations! No taste, nothing to see, nowhere to go, nothing to do, nowhere to travel! Your whole point, your whole purpose if you like, is to have conversations with everyone else to evolve yourself to wherever you need to go, to understand, to resolve, to do whatever you've got to do. You've got access to all the information of their past life.

And the minute you speak to them, they can see everything you've done in every single past life. They don't see the whole thing. They don't get a download all at once. He told me that. He said, "But they have access to it". So you know, you're talking to somebody and then suddenly in the middle of this conversation they say something and you're like, "Oh I know what you mean I can see that you did that" and they can actually see. That's where they are seeing everything you've done. And they say, "Oh yeah I get that now". He said that's all they're doing. They're interacting...

Hubby: Wow.

Me: So they're connecting, they're communicating, they're seeing everything. He told me this, "Every single thing you've done and will do, every body will see in their conversations with you. Nothing is hidden, everything is seen. Everything matters". He said, "Everything you do now - it matters. Even if people don't understand it now. Your soul will continue to evolve in incarnated form back to earth". It will keep coming, it will keep going. Eventually, you know, everybody's greatest fears and all that kind of stuff about the earth doesn't matter because the end process is this. We all evolve past physical right? So it's not required. The depression thing he said, "You would be surprised how common that it is at this stage. Because people have to work through a lot of stuff to get past attachments and purpose and all that. So never judge anyone". And he did say, "You don't need to get to this stage. You actually don't need to get to this stage to not have another incarnation. It's just a stage that some people have to get to. It's not for everybody, you don't have to. Some people are way evolved past this stage already here (meaning on our earth)". He said, "Don't judge anyone on your planet for having depression, because that could be their final stage of incarnation". And he did say that to me. And he is talking about humanity. This is humanity that he's talking about right? Even though one would say he's an alien but he would say, "No, this is humanity. This is. Everything that you've learned about humans - it's relevant". Everything that we've gone through here, there are many other universes going through the same stages because this is humanity. And it's evolving and it's a consciousness, what we are experiencing. And it's a relevant consciousness, yeah? And he was, if you like, human. I was talking to another human, but in a different form. And he said, "I'm not dead. I'm alive". He said, "The paradox of our universe is an interesting one".

Hubby: His universe?

Me: Yes, his universe – ours we'll get to - but his universe. He said, "The paradox of our universe is an interesting one in that we are in Spirit form yet we are not dead". Yet it's very similar to our universe (earth) where we are at where we have the 3D, people are deceased and they're hanging around. He said, "Don't get confused by it", haha, "if you can! but it's different. We are not all dead. We are alive in a different form. Last incarnation". So anyway… it was huge. He told me lots of stuff – personal stuff as well. How wonderful you are and how creative you are as well and like it hasn't even started yet.

At the ending of sharing this with my hubby I realised that interesting the story of creation in the bible begins with, "In the beginning was the Word, and the Word was with

God". And I felt the irony that in the end all we have is conversations to help us back to peace. "In the end is the word, and the word is with God".

Later that day hubby and I reflected a bit more on the meditation and I recorded it.

Me: It all makes sense.

Tony: It's so logical. Sounds like, why wouldn't it be like that, almost?

Me: I know and the more you reflect on it, the more it feels like, "Of course that would be the last step". And as I was writing it this morning I heard, "In the beginning was the word and in the end is the word". That's all you've got left, these conversations you're having with people. You know the story of creation how it says "In the beginning was the word and the word was God" in the bible?

Hubby: I'm not totally familiar with that.

Me: Oh right okay, well that's the creation story, interestingly enough.

Hubby: Yeah right.

Me: The beginning of consciousness it's like is the word and at the end of consciousness in the end there's the word.

Hubby: Yeah.

Me: I've got so many questions though. Like, what happens when there's only one soul left? You know, like, do they have any help? What happens, like how does that work? And is that place that I...that I...

Hubby: You're assuming there is an end to souls.

Me: Well that's true...I was just thinking just then as I was saying it, that portal that I got to at the end maybe that's the last step. Maybe that's where the last soul is. They're talking to other people that come through that little portal because there's no one in that universe left but then you said what's the point of these universes, well maybe the point is that...

Hubby: No, I didn't say, "What's the point of the Universes".

Me: Oh.

Hubby: I said, "What's the point of the Flower of Life Mandala - The tunnel, to connect the Universes together?", you know?

Me: That's what I just said, maybe that's the point that if there's only one soul left and they're not quite finished then who do they converse with? And maybe that's the point of the tunnel that they need to converse with someone outside of the universe from another universe.

Hubby: Yeah, that's right.

Me: There has to be a help, there's always a help, that's the Unity Principle. That we're all connected and we're never alone.

Hubby: So that's in that specific universe.

Me: That's right, exactly, in that specific universe.

Hubby: There's a lot to take in, there's so many different theological and scientific processes you could apply to it. It's neither scientific or theological or anything like that. It's fits in sort of both doesn't it?

Me: Uhuh.

Hubby: Interested to hear more from Ralph.

Me: Yeah me too.

Hubby: Who's to say now that you've found 1 particular universe that you won't be exposed to other universes?

Me: But I was exposed to 2 others at the beginning of the week, but I didn't enter them, I was just shown them. But they were like, 1 was crystalline and 1 had a flying creature that looked like it was under water but it was flying. So I kind of feel like perhaps I could explore those, but I don't know if I'd get the consciousness of the same level of consciousness that I'm at, at the moment. Because the conversation that I had was distinctly human and he was talking about humanity and we're not the only humanity. Yeah, like, life is out there but.

Hubby: And also, that space travel and all this sort of stuff. You know, like, how you could possibly travel across the universe due to the distances involved. But, this is how you do it. You go within, instead of going without. You've got to go within, through the Flower of Life Mandala tunnels, which are aka worm holes.

Me: Yeah, well you could call them a worm hole.

Hubby: Yeah and that's how Interstellar Beings, that's the only way they can communicate when you think about it. Because physically the distance it's just too immense for a...

Me: Maybe it's created that way on purpose.

Hubby: Yeah.

Me: I'm gonna ask these questions to Ralph actually.

Hubby: Ralph's gonna be a busy little boy.

Me: Yeah, hahha, I'm excited.

Hubby: I would be too. So, is it like, are you able to go through the Flower of Life Mandala consciously at will.

Me: I don't know I haven't tried yet.

Hubby: Or is it only during that state of meditation?

Me: I will try it later today and see what happens.

Later that day hubby and I chatted some more...

Hubby: Is what you're saying when we die, we go to that Universe, our soul goes to that universe or it's completely separate to us?

Me: No, it's completely separate. However Ralph and I had a conversation that we had a contract that I would meet him in his universe.

Also later that day. I voiced recorded many questions whilst sitting on the beach with hubby but for some reason they disappeared – only to be found a little later on down the road of this book. I thought at the time that it must be meant to be more of an organic process. And I got preoccupied with things and didn't go back in to talk to Ralph. But the Flower of Life Mandala called me again a few days later...

CHAPTER 3

Everything Matters

18 April 2018 — Conversation 2

I awoke at 5.30am to my spinning Flower of Life Mandala. I was told to be prepared. So I went to the loo, had a drink of water, jumped back into bed and started the voice recorder. I am recording the experience live as I'm experiencing it and describing it verbally as I go. This is a new experience for me. A real time one.

I go through the mandala, but no purple today. I immediately recognise that I've started off in a different universe. I am out the other side and in outer space. It's a different universe but feels familiar.

Me: I feel like I'm right at the edge of a planet, a big one. Why am I here?

Them: To Show you that multiple universes exist.

Me: There is beauty and life on other planets just like on earth. Feels familiar. Feels like I am on earth, but I am not. A bit like in the new, 'Lost In Space' movie — but a little bit different. There are animals, saw a flying bird like a tetradactyl but it wasn't - they tell me - but similar. Dinosaur-ish. I am getting it's more the timeline of Neolithic man. Humans definitely evolving from certain bone structure characteristics that pertain to a certain level of consciousness that mimic the ape but are not the ape — but similar. The forms of the bones are formed. I am being told that I'm being taken to this universe because they want me to be prepared for a visit to Ralph next…to be in some kind of rhythm with how I'm going stay focused while I am recording. And they're calling me back now. I feel a nervousness and the base of my spine tingling and I feel in my stomach a bit, there's a bit of fear and weird feeling in my tummy. So...it's not about the place I'm in, it's about the next step. So...I'm going to come back now...I think...or am I going to go straight there? I don't know. I'm going to see...I see the purple light from this end of the tunnel and I'm through. Ralph's here. It's just energy. I've got my eyes slightly open actually. I asked him how he was. He's good and looking forward to my visit and he's glad I'm voice recording this. I'm going ask this question...

Me: What's the difference between being dead and being here?

Ralph: There's a big difference. Being dead means you still have many incarnations or haven't transitioned fully back to the spirit world, where you meet with the High Council and chart your next life and evaluate your previous life. This is a helpful space of respite before you return. Being here is the last incarnation and the finalisation of all that needs to be finalised, realised, resolved. The power of seeing every incarnation, that one has experienced, in another person - we have that capability here. We cannot see it in ourselves (fully) without interacting with another. This brings the power of unity consciousness to the fore. In unity we expand and only in unity do we expand at the final stage. Many have not realised this yet. They don't have the information I'm giving you and that is why it leads to depression and closes them off. There's much healing to do there in self-forgiveness and non-judgment of other people and what they see in other people. They do not understand the point of being here or this last step. In the Spirit world you can see everything. You can see everything you've ever experienced, from every life time. You're evaluating yourself and planning what you need next and you know that you need others to fully realise we are one. And Tony asked, "What is the point of all this?". Many ask and that is why they get stuck in depression. But the point is - we can't do it alone. Even though we are all one. The true essence of oneness is that everything exists in oneness. And earth and our universe are examples of that. Many levels of everything. Creation, thought, feeling, rock, plant, earth, formation, mountain, weather, the multitude of combinations of everything put together, such as your principles (referring to the 12 Principles that I write about in the Everyday Lightworker Bible and several other books). You all come back to. It puts you together and it all puts us together. Integration of everything is the purpose. The power in that is huge and that is why, without mentioning names, that you've already thought of, when people speak to you and they say that, "Everything is not a mirror" and "That's all bullshit", that you recoil. That you cannot resonate with anyone promoting disconnection and denial that we are all one. And on a personal note, you know why you've left certain things that don't feel like you are connecting on that level even though that 'Being' may be more evolved than you in certain aspects which is true. Perhaps they are able to, as their third eye is so highly developed, read the internal situation of a person's medical situation. However, as I've told you, this land, this non-land, this Universe is created with no 'body' yet we see everything. And so the next level is that. Many who have had that skill in their past lives find they are at a bit of a loss here, because when the Third Eye is developed but the unity consciousness is lacking they feel superfluous and they feel loss and they feel powerless.

Me: Ralph I thank you very much for that information because that explains a lot to me. I feel very grateful for you explaining that to me and I'm sure that that will make sense to a lot of people, I know it does to me. I have been shown that an awakened Third Eye does not equal certain principles that I live my life by. One of them being Unity. The other being Honesty and integrity about that. I've been shown that and I'm careful now of that and watching for that, especially given who my social network is. I want to know if it's my job to educate people on this? I don't know if I'm asking the right person, but I would like your feedback on whether you think I need to educate people on the lessons I'm learning with you as I go or whether I need to sit with the information and pen a book. What your feeling on that is, would be interesting to hear at the very least. And it is personal but I'd like to hear that information please if you have any feedback or input?

Ralph: Yes of course. You are here because you've been chosen to educate the world that you live in of things beyond their world - at this point in time. So, the people when they are at this level in your world, can transition fully into the oneness. Fully integrated. And there is no holding back of information at this stage. There is no reason to. There are many in your world on their final incarnation. Many who do not need to come here - many do not need to be stretched to the point where there is no body to understand the things that you've already learned. Such as yourself. However, you know that some of you choose to come back. Even if you are fully integrated, you always have the choice to be that person. And you have been chosen in your next incarnation and you have seen this already that you will be working with the body in a medical situation as a Professor and you will be teaching medical intuition and medical - beyond, beyond what we are experiencing in this particular energetic vibration on earth. When I say 'we', I say 'we' as a humanity. And you know this, you've seen this, we've shown you this and I'm working in conjunction with your guides. And when I say 'we', that is because when you are at this level, when you don't have a body you can observe very easily what is going on with those people that you are contracted with and are required to assist. And so I can easily bilocate to your Universe at any time and I can easily see what you are ready for and what you have learned. And that is why you have been called here. It's time.

Me: Okay, I understand that. I understand that. It makes sense to me. What I'm understanding is that and this is a question, but in our earth Universe where we have this opportunity to evolve, it will evolve eventually to a non-physical state because that is required for some souls to evolve?

Ralph: That is correct, that is correct. And Tony asked, "Is there other universes?" Of course there are. And, "What's the point?" That's because there are many souls that are required to be in that experience right now. Whereas on earth they are not. And, "Do they incarnate in a different universe if they are ready for that?" Not required, because the experiences that they have had within their own, create a karmic tie, if you like, to that world. Where they have experienced, numerous times, many relationships with those individuals that once, at this point of where we are in this bodiless form, they are required to be triggered to learn to process. Like I said, we are processing all the time here. There is nothing left than the memories and the feelings and the Spirit/soul connection of evolving past and beyond into full acceptance and unity and connection without angst, without triggers. With just peace - that highest vibrational frequency that met you when you asked, "What is the highest vibrational frequency?", when you arrived here. So yes, there are many universes each unto their own. But having said that, as you know, you and a few others have been chosen to travel to learn and to take back information so in essence, the unity connection is still there. That one universe cannot evolve without the other, is part of the intrinsic nature of unity. So, you have a job to do. Part of that job is informing earth of these messages. Those that are ready will feel validated and amazing, just as you did today, and you were quite teary and you know how it felt to be validated on that level. Think about that. Think about how people will feel when they hear this information. When they too have experienced what you have and felt humiliated because they (others) could see clearer in some respects to you on a physical level. But think about it. The impulse behind everything is energetic. The impulse behind everything is energetic. It can be read. But only up to the level that the person understands and connects with the highest vibrational frequencies. To distinguish the high, we must also be able to distinguish the low. To distinguish the low, we must have a connection and feeling and understanding and energetic intelligence on how that serves us. One must have a high sense of their Higher Self in order to reflect on that level. One must be willing to embrace the 'shadow' as you call it. All those aspects of the personality that we deem shameful, bad etc. If they aren't owned, they are not only disowned and manifest in other ways, but they aren't seen. And when we don't want to see them, that cuts the Third Eye off on an energetic level from what can be seen moving forward past this 3D existence.

Me: Okay, makes a lot of sense. I see, so the clarity of the Third Eye is like, tuned in almost like a radio station to this 3D world? Which I can understand, which is really great if you are still seeing the 'physical'.

Ralph: If they are looking for the issue for another person, they can find it. And if that's part of their job to look for the energetics behind the 3D world, they can find it - they will find it. And they can evolve their Third Eye through that process.

Me: Okay I see, yep ok. So that's a very deep thing to understand. And I guess I honestly have not walked that path of developing my Third Eye on a physical level to be able to see inside the body like they do to that level of detail - I haven't. And I'm being shown by you that that's my next life time in the medical field hence why I have had medical intuitive experiences here and have had that sort of energetic connection as a precursor to that.

Ralph: Not everybody has the energetic connection of the empathic feelings before they can see inside the body. For some people that comes later. For you it's a skill that you can develop moving forward in the future that is not necessary to learn how 'this place' serves you to understand where you're moving towards. It is not required. But you are learning and understanding how to work with those who have this issue, in your next incarnation. And to help to bridge that gap. And that is your Professor status. It is not merely about the medical. You are bringing forward, you are developing in this life time of course developing this insight, but in the next time, mastering it. So, there are levels of what you do in each life time and what, in the nature of time, you can achieve in one life time. And Tony asked about time, "Is there time in this world?" Yes, there is time. Although we don't have the sun rising and we don't have the sun setting, there is a lot of time and interaction that exists between us. That's why people get depressed. Because it seems it's endless. Yet in peace, when peace is endless, you're in bliss. You're in joy and you're in celebration. And every time I see someone resolve something, because I can read, and we at this level we can read how many are close to that point, there is an incredible feeling of joy. You know how that feels and you can feel it in your heart right now? You know how it feels Michelle. When you see someone overcome something and resolve something. There is no greater feeling is there? And that's what motivates you to do the job that you do. Well, it's true here. And I know you're feeling emotional and it's affecting your voice box and that's how much joy we feel here, seeing people. And you asked the question, "How do we die here, there's no body?" We don't, we 'resolve'. And as I said to you, there is a lot of depression here. Why? When people just disappear on you because they're 'resolved' and you're not required to 'resolve' in this plain with that person and there is no return of that soul, in midway plain, like on your earth, the only thing left is grief. And that grief can be endless for someone who has an attachment to 'resolving' that which can't be 'resolved' as you know on earth. You have mediumship on earth. We have no mediumship here. The only mediumship we have is between 2 people. Or a group of souls who come together to talk about certain topics and we do have that to help each other resolve. Not everybody understands the purpose of resolving. And it can be a very painful time for some people in this universe. Those that are evolved as myself, can see all for that person and understand all and be in complete compassion and joy that they're 'almost there'. I cannot describe to you the process in intricate detail, but I will. I want to. But it's enough to take in for you to process in your period of time, in your world, all the information that I've given you. I want to reiterate something to you Michelle. Everything matters. You come to me in this world through the portal to connect, to have the experience of being here. Yet you do not have to. You can call me there. I've been with you whole time off and on through your life, as one of your guides. You're used to speaking to me. And as your guides don't usually have faces - you're clairaudient and you don't mind where Spirit's talking to you from - I have been used in many occasions to help you. And that is why I feel so familiar to you. I'm not Archangel Michael but I'm very familiar with him. And we work together. And I work with him. Things are going to change for your dramatically soon. Your world will feel upside down. May this be your constant to know, everything matters. Even when you don't understand it. With everything you are going through right now that's the strongest message I can give you and I'll leave you with that.

Me: Okay, thank you Ralph I really appreciate everything you've said to me today. That's huge information to take in and I do appreciate it and I'm very grateful, very grateful and I know last time I was here you gave me a hug and it was a weird warm fluid sensation was sinking into my skin and as you were embracing me and I just wanted to say I really enjoyed that. Here's another one I'm getting it. (Hugging ensues) It's a Oneness Hug. It went all the way through me that time. That's beautiful. Last time it was only half.

Ralph: That's because you were more in the energy of wondering what it felt like than in the hug.

Me: That's true, this time I really wanted to let it in. Thank you, Ralph. I will see you next time, maybe I'll try calling you forward in this world. So...I don't need to chat with you in your world in order to experience the communication that I have with you. Thank you.

Ralph: You're welcome. Now Go and Share.

Me: I will.

I travelled back through the worm whole. Purple light on the tunnel. Like I was walking through it rather than being pulled along. I'm back.

CHAPTER 4

The Sauna Chat

19 April 2018 — Conversation 3

My husband Tony and I decided to have a sauna and see whether I could call Ralph to me with him there. The following is a transcribe of the recording.

Me: Let's see if we can contact Ralph. He's saying he's here and we can both talk to him.

Tony: Hmm…I forget what I was going to say now.

Me: Welcome to my world.

Tony: Yes, welcome to our universe.

Me: No, I was talking to you.

Tony: Oh!

Me: Hahahaha, I forget too, I forget too. You were going to ask him about demons weren't you? Today when we were watching the film.

Tony: That's right yeah. So, are demons that we interpret in this universe basically just, not nice beings from other universes?

Michelle: No, no. What I'm hearing him say is that each universe has their own energetic lower vibrations and higher vibrations. So, it's not necessary for any beings of a lower vibrational nature to travel through the portals to serve a purpose for catalyst for change within our universe.

Tony: Uhuh.

Me: So we have them unto our own universe.

Tony: So are there multiple spiritual universes or is there just one spiritual plane?

Me: So, the universes are separate to the spiritual plane.

Tony: Yeah, that's not what I'm asking.

Me: There are multiple universes and they are all separate to the spiritual plane.

Tony: Yes, that's not what I'm asking. Is the spiritual plane a single plane or is their multiple spiritual universes?

Me: No just the ALL. You've got 4 levels. You've got all levels that evolve humanity. Which is our universe, our style of universe and also his, that eventually becomes bodiless and formless. You've got in between realm where people can actually communicate who are in between zone between here and their respite. Third you've got the rest and planning for their next incarnation zone. And then you've got the place where people go to when they resolve, which is back into the ALL because they are fully integrated.

Tony: Ask him what do we need to know right now?

Ralph: You're doing really well in coping with the information, working as a team, working things through, integrating what you can, not judging yourselves for what you can't right now and keep turning up and communicating to get information that you need.

Me: And he'll be there.

Tony: Ask him if he has sex in his universe.

Ralph: No, joy.

Tony: They don't?

Me: No, no sex. Healing, a lot of sexual healing but no sex.

Tony: Oh…

Me: Connecting on an energetic level, hugs and those kind of things but not, obviously intercourse because there is no body.

Tony: Ask him is he able to see into our future?

Ralph: Yes, that's easy but there's always a choice, so you can change your future….

Tony: Yeah, I'm not asking…

Me: He's talking, I'm just letting him talk.

Ralph: Yes, we can see into your future easily.

Tony: Ask him what's the best way for mankind to find peace.

Ralph: To resolve anything they need to, to be fully integrated.

Tony: Ask him if the portals are the only way that people can transverse universes.

Ralph: Yes, initially and then once the awareness is there, they can actually just literally be where they know they've connected to.

Tony: Ask him if he has met any other beings from this universe besides from this planet.

Me: Yes, but he's only been assigned a few to mentor through this process, not all. There are others like him helping as well.

Tony: Yeah. So, ask him if there's many civilized or evolved beings on different planets in this universe.

Ralph: Yes.

Tony: Are we able to physically travel to these planets?

Ralph: Yes.

Tony: What was that?

Me: Yes, technology wise not yet, but yes it's a capability.

Tony: Yeah physically, it's possible.

Me: Yes but it's a capability. Just he's showing me that its just not possible to survive through worm holes because it's a complete energy shift. So, it's like a death, so if someone goes down a worm hole they die. Technically they don't survive it.

Tony: Does he know what happens to our souls when we die?

Me: Yeah, just that we always have a choice to chart our next life with more specifics after we've done 2 things. First that we've allowed ourselves to hang around for as long as we feel is required in the middle plane to communicate with our loved ones. And specifically watch over them. And then go to the next zone where we are planning our next incarnation and the things that we feel we need to learn to evolve to as far as we feel we can evolve to, however we can surpass that once we are back here on earth.

Tony: Ask him if Jesus Christ was a visitor from another universe.

Ralph: Jesus Christ was a consciousness that happens in every single universe that exists because the Christ consciousness is a consciousness that we all evolve to. Different man, different form, whatever, but consciousness-wise the same. And there are many versions of Jesus in respect to different civilizations across time. For instance, Buddha. Similar message. Christ, similar message. Different ends, but required for consciousness to evolve at different ends of the planet to bring everybody up at the same point. Internet is speeding this up significantly.

Tony: Ask him if it's possible for me to use one of the portals.

Ralph: Yes.

Tony: Ask him how.

Me: Well he's telling me that you know about them now.

Tony: Right, so how.

Me: Second hand information doesn't require you to have to 'try' you can just choose to. He's showing me you can sit down, close your eyes, walk through the portal, have the intention to be where you want to be in his universe and then actually arrive. It's not required to be called there. And also for people who haven't had my experience to be called there doesn't mean they're not worthy to go there or explore that. They can freely do that if they wish.

Me: I want to ask about something. Unless you have another question…

Tony: No I can't think of anything. I was trying to find the portal.

Me: Oh, were you, sorry. Maybe I'll just leave you to that or a little while.

Tony: Okay.

I gave Tony some space and turned off voice recorder for a bit.

Me: So I asked Ralph about people on other planets in this universe whether they're human or not. And he said there are different levels of consciousness of humanity within the same universe. But those expressions of humanity may look like a different race, like a different looking creature that may well be more evolved than us and yet they're not 'not human'. They're still human. And when some of them are incarnating into this human body they feel like they are weird but the reason why they are here is for 2 reasons. Firstly, is to experience what it's like to be in a human body, at that evolved state so that evolves them even further - because it's very challenging apparently, being in a human body. The second is to assist humanity to evolve so that there is help within the human race, helping itself from another level of consciousness. But it's a bit like for them coming here, a backward step but not, because its required for their progression. However, it's a bit like being an ape being born into a dog form where it's like you're going backwards or it feels weird. It doesn't feel like yourself. You don't have the capability that you used to. You can't do the things that you used to. And so there's a struggle and challenge with those particular star beings that we choose to call them here on earth. Or could be, we might think they're aliens. However, having said that there are beings that more evolved that have still not resolved or integrated certain aspects, so they practise the darker side of humanity still, in a more evolved form. And that's what people talk about when they feel they may have been interfered with or abducted, or things like that. And the best protection is to be as resolved and integrated in yourself as possible as a human being, so that you repel those shadow aspects that you could possibly attract when you are unconscious. And this can relate to previous past lives as well and so therefore it can be, if you like, karmic attraction to the darkness, even at a very young age as a child. But having said that it's not set in concrete because many children have to experience these things because they have big jobs here to do to help humanity evolve. Sometimes a very young child will chart something very nasty to happen to them before they come here so that at a later time they can help humanity. Even people around them going through what has happened with that child, can evolve. And they act as a sacrifice if you like for the greater good. What do you think of all that?

Tony: Oh, I was not listening honey, I was trying to…

Me: Oh, you weren't listening!

Tony: ..get my mandala happening.

Me: Sorry, you don't need to see the mandala.

Tony: Oh.

Me: Remember, he said you don't have?

Tony: What do you have to do?

Me: Just have the intention to go through the worm hole, just imagine one, and set the intention that you're walking through the worm hole and out the other side is their universe.

Tony: Oh.

Me: That's it, you don't have to look for the mandala.

Tony: Oh, I thought you had to get the mandala first to get the worm hole.

Me: No!

CHAPTER 5

Earth Calling Ralph

20 April 2018: Conversation 4

I decided to call Ralph to me.

Me: So people can see in the future in your land?

Ralph: Yes.

Me: So why would there be depression for those who don't understand the point of resolving?

Ralph: There is angst towards God, towards the process. They haven't experienced the peace of resolving, integrating, one thing consciously. Can you imagine what that must be like?

Me: Wow, you mean seriously there's people who haven't consciously tried to do anything for their personal development?

Ralph: Yes, because they may well have contracted in a previous time to be that person who was the catalyst for everyone else.

Me: I'm very confused. I don't understand.

Ralph: Let's talk about the grief process first and it might help you understand. When I said that people just 'disappear' because they've resolved…it can be unexpected. And there is a lot of loss. And there may be well someone who judges that process as 'wrong'. However, it is required because if abandonment isn't triggered, and that's one of the deepest triggers, if abandonment isn't required, isn't achieved, isn't triggered, then the person cannot deal with their or build their connection with God. Yes, we are psychic here in so far as we can see the ramifications of decisions with our Third Eye. Some of us have evolved to the point we can see what people have charted and with who. However, being an evolved being, and I reiterate this to you, does not remove you from depression. Depression is the last stop in really dealing with one's connection to the Higher Power, the All, the All knowing. There is only one thing that can solve abandonment really on the deepest level and that is reconnection with Higher energy, higher frequency. That's the only solution. Some people get that with a conversation with God. Some people get that with a conversation with guides. Some people get that from changing their mind, their thoughts, to more loving thoughts, gratitude, peace and acceptance etc. But they cannot resolve this grief of being in depression, which is being in the stagnant part of grief, not a grief that they have moved through. They cannot resolve this unless they learn to reconnect to these higher frequencies. That they trust them is the key. That they trust 100% is the key. And when they don't trust, it's still a base chakra issue even though there is no body and there's no chakras, it's still energetically they're stuck on that lower frequency.

Me: So…can I just confirm what you just said. So basically, they are in this land and they may have been an evolved being. They have contracted to be the trigger - on some level they know this. They also know that they are yet to build that connection as strongly as they need to for themselves or something? I'm not sure, why would they plan it? Why would they be in the high council with that awareness and come back to this final incarnation without that awareness?

Ralph: Because in the Spirit world when you are talking to the High Council you see what holds you back. You see where your vulnerabilities are. You are once removed as it were. You're a little bit like, you see all the wounds, you have a respite from your conscious evolving self and you have the insight for that moment with your council guides to actually see. You know what it takes. You know. You kind of know what your pressure valve is. What will push you over the edge to have the realisation. You're in..not control..but in the box seat of really understanding 'you' and that is a unique position. Because even myself in this land, I may be able to bi-locate and even be a guide in another universe. And maybe I've evolved to that level, but I haven't evolved to the level where I can see everyone's trigger and where it is and how far they are to it. That's personal, that's very personal. And it's really none of my business as well. If we were able to see everyone's triggers and the solution to everyone's depression and how they can get there, that would be very co-dependent in a lot of ways because it would be that we were manipulating things for people to shift and to resolve. We would become addicted to their process instead of celebrating just how close they are because on an energetic level we can read that. We can read how close they are. On an energetic level we can read that there is a wound, there's something blocking them. On an energetic level we can tell you what that person's feeling if you like without the body, where they are vibrating, their frequency, in general their overall frequency. We are certainly able to read thoughts, that's how we communicate because we have no voice box. But are we able to tell you what would it take for this person to completely resolve? No, no we would not.

Me: I'm just going to stop this because I'm really affected by this garbage truck in the background.

Me: Okay, I see so, I lost a little bit of concentration there but…what I'm seeing and hearing…and by the way I can kind of, while you're talking I can. I'm in your universe but I am with you here so I'm getting a visual of what you are talking about and it is quite hard to understand what it would feel like to be that evolved and yet to still have that issue.

Ralph: Yep, but you are still judging depression. You are still judging a low vibrational frequency as bad or wrong. Being evolved does not mean that you don't have things that have been with you a very, very long time. Habits even, as it were. If they were, for example, someone who is so evolved that they were the only person that they could commit to being a catalyst for someone's change for many years, they played a role where they were so disconnected. In your world, you can associate it with psychopathic. So disconnected from feeling, so devoid of feeling, so empty, so robotic, so clinical, so able to commit the most heinous acts…to be that trigger, to really test people that they cannot trust a higher power because a higher power would not allow these things to happen. And then, they are in this realm, this last incarnation, where they know very well, they've charted that they do need if you like cleanse themselves from all the things that they have done, like a purification, if they have to face those things because the person that they've done those things too, their healing may only just be at that stage as well. And they need, the person that has had these heinous acts committed by this psychopath – has to see that the psychopath only did what they did to challenge them to be triggered. Now, that reminds the psychopath as well, who they are.

Me: I have a question, I'm going to interrupt here. How does the person who's been abused or killed in a heinous way or what have you…how do they know that this person has contracted with them. How do they have that realisation?

Ralph: That is an excellent question, because some of us resolve/integrate to the point where we can actually see our contracts. Remember when I told you, when you initially came here that we had contracted to do this? Well, it may only take one person who has contracted with this psychopath to trigger that for them, for them to understand how incredibly selfless they've been in charting such horrendous life times. It may only take one for this person to remember who they are and to restore their vibration however, in my experience I have seen, psychopaths in particular - because they have been so disconnected from feelings and especially without a body - it can be even harder to understand and have that realisation consciously "why would I even do that?", that it takes them a lot of time. It's almost like an ice cube melting and that doesn't take 2 seconds in the sun. Sometimes it takes a while to melt. And in a cooler climate where there's no sun if you like and perhaps an endless array of souls that this person has affected, it can be extraordinarily depressing for them.

Me: How is it solved that they would… I'm seeing that it's about self-forgiveness or something, I don't understand it.

Ralph: Like I told you earlier there is a lot of self-forgiveness required here. When I mentioned to you that…

Me: I'm being shown a whole process here, it's very hard to keep up with the speaking. He's showing me that when they're meeting in the high council and the psychopath is making that decision and then he's back in the last incarnation and he's wondering how he could have done that to himself, there's almost a self-hatred there for how he could treat himself like that. So it's like the relationship with his conscious self in the spirit world and how he could do what he does, there's like this huge gap, like a real big conflict.

Ralph: Yes, that is correct and it's very hard to describe how that could be a possibility. When you have an evolved being. But as I said to you, this is the last port. This is the last incarnation. You can be evolved with all your other chakras, all your other energy systems as a human being, but if your base chakra issue is not resolved it can affect everything. That trust and that safety aspect of connection to spirit, that box must be ticked in order to fully resolve. And not everybody has that particular issue here. Not everybody has depression here before they resolve. In fact, they may be here a long time and move from depression to other aspects of their energetic system before they resolve. It may take them some time to shift, however, it's not the last port of call before you resolve. Not everybody has that particular issue. So it's very important to understand that.

ฉ 46 ฉ

Me: I do understand that. So you're just giving me an example.

Ralph: Yes, that's right. I'm giving you an example of the hardest type of grief to resolve…is the abandonment of self or the perceived abandonment of self and the perceived abandonment of God or higher energies and judgement of those things and inability to understand. But it's simple. If the universe is everything, is all, then a complete expression of all that must be accepted. Even the darkest aspects. Because if we leave any dark bits out, if we judge any darkness then we are literally judging ourselves and disconnecting from that. How can we be integrated? So you see, you need to really go through all those things in those life times. You need to be every 'thing', every expression in order to completely integrate. And for those people who think they haven't been the expression of being a rapist, a paedophile, a murderer, a con artist, a fraudulent person, a cheater, an addict of any kind…no, you will do it all. All of you. All of you will do it all. You will do it all. You will forgive it all. You will integrate it all and you will resolve.

(When my husband read this on 3 May 2018, he questioned whether we all had to BE everything in order to integrate it. When I heard him question this, I received more clarity on how Ralph was talking about it as an 'expression'. That we would all experience the 'expression' of these archetypes. For example, we have taken advantage of innocents by abusing our power (paedophile), we have been deceptive of our authenticity (fraudulent), we have lied to people (con artist), we have killed others' ideas with our closed mind (murderers), we have violated people's boundaries by imposing our will on others (rapist). The key to integration rests with facing and accepting all these aspects of ourselves with 100% compassion. To help us get there we can ask ourselves certain questions. How do we feel about those parts of ourselves and our behaviour? Have we come to a place of understanding and peace with ourselves? How resolved are we with our actions? Have we learned from those behaviours that we are in fact equal with others? Do we have 100% compassion for the parts of ourselves that committed these acts? What has that darker, denser side to our nature taught us about ourselves? When we are able to come to a place of understanding and compassion for ourselves, then we can integrate the darker aspects and know the value that they have played in the lives of ourselves and others. We can also then be at peace with people that have been paedophiles, murderers, con artists, fraudulent person, etc to us. We can have 100% compassion for them and in doing so, we are resolved.)

Me: Okay, that's a lot! But thank you Ralph I really appreciate it and I'm going to have to get going now but thank you.

Ralph: Well thank you very much for listening and passing this information on so quickly to people. And don't worry about who's downloaded the dropbox folder - of all the information I've told you so far - off facebook please. Don't worry about that. You've done what you need to do. And those who are curious, and those who need to be activated, they will be reading it. But you've fulfilled your duty of passing on that information and when I say duty I mean the action that you know to be something you can't hold onto right now. It's not responsible. It's only responsible to keep handing that information out and adding to it as you go. Know that it is extraordinarily important for some people to hear this right now. Not in a little while when you've finished a book on it and it sounds like that's what you are doing.

Me: Yes, I am doing that. I've started typing because I didn't know how else to communicate everything and integrate everything myself without rewriting and rehearing it and everything and so I started it and it's helped me, actually. It's the right decision. I find my throat chakra not being able to find the words as quickly as I thought I might when I'm out of a meditative state with you because for some reason this is so vast, that I kind of struggle. So I feel like I need to write it down in order to really grasp it myself and to even have clarity in talking to someone, that I have this safety net that I can kind of read it if I need to or something like that.

Ralph: I understand. You've got to go.

Me: I do, alright, lots of love, big hug. Thank you, great hug.

I went for a walk and recorded some reflections that I wanted to include in this process as it felt like it's something I could run past Ralph.

Me: Just having some insight into rehabilitation for prisoners who have killed people. Like they're not in communication with them. So perhaps in the future it will include mediumship. So the person who that they've actually killed can actually communicate with them. Not from a place of angst perhaps, in terms of shaming them or what have you, but from a place of developing connection. Not developing, as we would call it the 'conscience', but developing a connection with people in unity. So, taking them out of the 'good' and 'bad' and 'right' and 'wrong' and being more in the connection with people.

CHAPTER 6

Birthday Bomb

21 April 2018: Conversation 5

I awoke on my birthday to a conversation with Ralph and wanted to share it with Tony via a voice recording so I wouldn't lose the precious learnings so early in my day. Ralph dropped a bomb about an epidemic we have at the current time that is contributing to suicides.

Me: So anyway, I had this conversation this morning. It's my birthday – just saying – and I don't want to lose it before I tell you. It's pretty clear. It's pretty clear though. He was talking about 'walk ins'.

Tony: Walk-Ins?

Me: You know how some people say they're a walk in?

Tony: No.

Me: No, you haven't heard that, okay? So…walk-ins are when people have one personality one day and then the next they have a completely different personality and they have access to all these talents that they never had and they're completely, like a different person. He was talking about how people from the bodiless universe that he lives in who know about other universes at that point and who are frustrated at not having a body, can come through the worm hole and they can actually take over someone's body, like a possession and it's like the host is in a coma asleep. And he said what they're doing in essence, they're not going to incarnate back into that universe, but they will not be able to resolve in his universe alone. So technically they won't incarnate into a bodily form, but if they don't resolve all their karmic ties they're creating from taking over as a host in another universe with a body, they're creating an issue there where they have to resolve in that universe as well at the end. Right?

Tony: Right...uhuh.

Me: So this is what they're doing, in essence, they're creating a situation for themselves where they have to also wait a long time until, if they don't resolve...They've created for themselves a little bit of a mess. Because people that they affect, they have to hang round karmically for these other people, to resolve. So they're creating a situation of delay for themselves and others. Does that make sense?

Tony: Uhuh.

Me: Really?

Tony: Yes.

Me: And I can see it. I can see it as I'm talking to you. They're frustrated. They're quite evolved, but they're frustrated not having a body and so they've worked out that they can do this, come through. But what they don't understand is, they're creating karmic ties to both universes and they can't resolve over there...

Tony: Well there not there.

Me: No but they can't resolve over there alone. Even if their host eventually passes, and they've delayed the..they've actually interfered with the contracts that particular host has made with people and they're actually creating a bit of a delay for them and also a bit of chaos for the contracts that have been put together for that life, for a number of people. So it's a boundary issue. It's a boundary violation. It creates another element in the mix of what we call, what's the word for it, I'm trying to work it out. Interference with destiny almost. Even if you're destined to meet this person in your life because you contracted it, it's been side-swiped.

Tony: Diverted.

Me: Uhuh, for that particular life time. Which is a bit random. It's like a random thing. And what happens then is...and he's showing me...that obviously they're at their last incarnation there when that host dies, they can attach to another person! And literally continue to do that, which is a fricking long time. It's like living 2 universes worth of it evolving to that point where you don't have a body. That's a long time.

Tony: Hmmm.

Me: And he's saying what they can do is choose not to do that again. And then they can choose to come back to his universe and resolve as much as they can there.

Tony: Seems such a stupid thing to do for someone who's supposed to get to the highest realm in their universe. To me it doesn't make sense that these beings are supposed to be incarnated in this highest realm in their universe where they don't need a body and everything to get to that point and then they go and do something like that. It seems to me if that's where their minds at, how did they get to be in that last realm, you know?

Me: Yeah, he said that the base chakra level is the hardest bit. That's the hardest bit so that they're stuck with that, you know? And it is the God/trust connection, the base chakra. And yeah, if you don't get that, you are trying to control everything, you are trying to manipulate everything on a physical level. He was saying that there are a lot of walk-ins here at this current time and it's a bit epidemic. And so this kind of information needs to be told. So that the only way we can help them in their universe is to educate our universe about that so they stop doing that. But in order to be taken over by a walk-in, the only protection you've got, is being conscious and aware of yourself and being connected. So that's the only...you can't go into a coma if you've got a self-awareness level that's too aware, you know?

Tony: Mmm.

Me: So he said as soon as that person dies, oh and he is showing me as I'm speaking to you, that's how a lot of suicides occur. Because what's happened is the only way they can leave because they're so attached to the body, is to suicide. It's like they've lost the ability to be bodiless, almost and the only way out is to go, "I'm outa here". And so that's more information there on suicide. And that's why people say, "They weren't themselves". And that's why depression leads to suicide. They are being shown, they can't come here and expect to feel resolved because they've got a body back. They're not going to resolve the emotional stuff. Anyway, that's that. Any questions?

Tony: Oh, you already answered it.

Me: Oh.

CHAPTER 7

Intergalactic Nose Job

21 April 2018 — Conversation 6

Later that day a friend and I organised a call as she had some questions for Ralph and I agreed to see if Ralph would come through in 'real time' to answer her questions.

Me: So are you cool for me to record now?

Friend: Yeah, I'm cool!

Me: Awesome!

Friend: I've just jotted down a couple of things.

Me: Fabulous! I got so much information through this morning about so much and I'm really curious because I've already recorded that. Like I told Tony. So I already recorded that. So it will just be interesting to see what you ask as well.

Friend: Yes.

Me: Anyway, but what are your questions?

Friend: I've got them all ready. Do you want me to tell you them before we start?

Me: No, no, it's okay. You can do one at a time.

Friend: Okay. Just copying them down so I've got them in order.

Me: Yep.

Friend: Alright, I've got 4 main ones. I am ready!

Me: Okay, shoot from the hip baby!

Friend: Can you tell me more about why it is we get stuck in that state of depression and what's the gift?

Me: Yes, so a lot of people don't…that's a complex question because, especially because of the nature of what I learned this morning which was that some people try to escape their depression from that particular universe and they have actually found a way to come back on through, to our universe, and to desperately try to escape the endlessness of that reality. The depression is caused from what seems like an endless amount of time where you can't really escape yourself and you can't escape your issues. They're just in your face continually. So, if someone does not want to face their issues, they're going to want to escape and they can't. And so there's a depression that sets in. The only way they can kind of escape is to kind of go inward which creates this really big depression. But what I was shown this morning was that they can come over through, over here, and then take over a host and be like a 'walk-in' and try and live a life here. But what they are actually doing is creating karmic ties here. So in essence they're almost like, kind of sounds like prison really doesn't it? But it's almost like doubling the sentence. So they're creating - even though they don't come back into earth to incarnate - they are actually creating karmic ties that eventually when our universe evolves to that bodiless state, they're going to not only have to spend time resolving not only on one end of the universe but over here as well. They'll have more than one place they have to resolve. So they are actually creating a double amount. There's a big subject in that – I did a big recording on that, this morning that I'm going to write about anyway. Does that help?

Friend: Yes, yes.

Me: Great.

Friend: Okay, I'm interested in manifestation and instant manifestation. What are some key points about that around literally physically healing the body in a way that the body might be physically sick or you might be just physically manifesting changes in the body of greater health, growing younger, all those fun things.

Me: And it's really interesting – he's showing me – that even if they don't have the body there, there's still the instant manifestation of depression or avoidance or denial or whatever it is if you're not facing something - which is the precursor for all those illnesses. And so he's saying that the quickest way through to resolve anything that's a barrier to what you want – and so he's just saying "removing the barriers". Because your natural state of being is everything, is actually having everything. So he's just saying, "Don't think you have to do anything. Just resolve what's in the way from you having that perfect health".

Friend: This is a personal one. I have literally manifested healing on an issue of my nose. That sounds a bit out there and crazy, but I do believe I manifested help from that realm and they've literally sorted out my nose.

Me: Uhuh.

Friend: So am I way off?

Me: No, not at all. No, the actual thinking that you've got around certain topics, is that evolved level that they live by – that doesn't require being there (in their universe). A lot of them that have gotten to that point that are there, it's very evolved. So, what they're saying is, that ability doesn't exist merely on their level, you're creating that for yourself.

Friend: Because I literally woke up, with a cut line down my nose that didn't hurt at all. But it was this perfectly straight line. And all the issues were physically evident that had been fixed in my nose and I woke up in the morning. So am I on track?

Me: Yeah, so they're just saying that even if it feels like someone else has done this to you, it's still that you've been ready for that healing. Does that make sense?

Friend: Mmm.

Me: It's not even dependent on, "I put my order in for some angelic or intergalactic help to help me with my nose", that's not manifestation. They're saying just that the readiness to have it completely fixed is manifestation. And then that could come through anything. It could come through medical, it could come through intergalactic help, it can come through the angelic realm, it can come from the neurochemistry that we change inside our body as well. So, they're just saying it's simply one form or another. It will fix itself because there's no need for it anymore. You know the blockage and the barrier and everything that was going on in there, they're just saying, "You dealt with the emotional stuff behind it so there was no need to have it there anymore". Rather than you go out and get that fixed, if it required fixing, it's been done for you.

Friend: Did I do it? Did we do it – you guys and I? Or did I literally manifest it because where I was up to emotionally? Who did it? Did we do it? Did I do it? Did you guys do it?

Me: I'm just getting that it was something that was called in from a higher being. I'm feeling that the physical realm gets help all the time from the higher beings. It's not the job of the intergalactic beings in his universe to help our universe heal on a physical level. It's their job to help us to understand, because this is why he's communicating. It's their job to help us understand where the evolution of consciousness is getting to so that we can actually short cut it here. And so that people who are at that point, where they are perhaps at their last incarnation are not required to resolve any more, they can freely return then if they want to as spirit guides. They can do that, but they don't have anything more to resolve and he's saying there are many of you like that here, when you have experiences like that, it just validates you even further that anything is possible on that physical level. And that yes, that consciousness of resolving it follows through to the body. And the mechanisms and the machinations are wide and varied as to how that healing takes place. So, at the end of the day, it doesn't even matter. He's saying it doesn't really matter who did it. It's done. You don't have to worry about that. We're all connected in unity so it doesn't matter.

Friend: Right, good! I've got 2 more questions, the 3rd one is – I believe that we are all galactic beings in a huge galaxy and as I'm evolving in my consciousness, I sense that I've been meeting up with different ones of you guys since I was a child. In terms of my own safety been forgetting that and now remembering a lot of it and where I'm up to. Would I be right?

Me: Yeah, straight off the bat – I just get a sense of definitely – yes. It's interesting because he's saying...I will speak in a round about way to what he's saying so there is no pressure here. So he's saying...You know how we have memories surface from childhood that we might think aren't true and that other people might think untrue? He's just saying that the same goes for these kind of experiences - not just traumas - and we can start to unlock and activate and remember the memories, have also been the supportive memories. So, he's saying both can happen, both do happen and also the response of society to both the light and dark side can be quite invalidating. And he's saying that he's very happy that you're having them, and that you can validate yourself and that you're finding validation for them.

Friend: Okay...oh that's exciting! And a little tangent off that same question is, I'm excited to have more of what I think has no fear around it is the good memories with all of you guys.

Me: Yeah!

Friend: So because I feel like that, are those great memories going to come through more to me? Because I'm not fearful around it, I think it's exciting and it's only started in the last 8 months.

Me: Well he's just saying, "I'm happy to have direct contact with you". He's not working with too many people really. That's not his job. But there's a definite, what's it called, brotherhood, sisterhood, family feeling in terms of the communication and he just feels like you should know that. Feel free to contact him directly because he would be more than happy to converse with you and to maybe confirm some things that you need to clarify as well for your own experiences. And he's saying like he's really there and willing to be available for you.

Friend: Thank you. Because I'm excited. I have a strong sense now and it's getting stronger and stronger. I know I'm here to learn what I'm supposed to learn, but I want to meet my galactic family. Because I think that is my main family and I've just been plopped here to do what I've been meant to do. But there's yearning in my heart to find the love of that galactic family.

Me: I feel that's what he's showing me. There's definitely karmic ties within this universe that we have, but then there's a greater sense of that you've crossed universes for this kind of information to be activated internally in your body at certain periods of time as you've gone through. And there is a sense that there is something unique for you in all this. So, I'm excited to see how that unfolds for you because it does feel like family – it's almost like across universes family.

Friend: Yeah.

Me: So it's really nice, it's really lovely.

Friend: Oh, cool. And then the last one I have, although I could go on forever with this but these are the 4 main ones. You know I'm wresting with 2 sides of…Do we have a contract to complete and resolve? Or can we fast track that and the quicker we come into love and light, with whatever we are trying to resolve, the contract gets deleted and we can do that slow or fast.

Me: So, he's saying that the contract is 2 sided it's not just one-sided.

Friend: Ah…

Me: So, it's about feeling in to what the other person's – what the contract is for them – not just what it is for you. So, he's looking at it from the point of view of what does that actually look like for them? If they are not in a position where they can be resolved in this life time, part of that contract might be that you do indeed have to get on with things and do what you've got to do, without them in your space, for that contract to ride itself out properly. Because part of that contract might be that you get on with it and that person's watching your life from a distance and can only learn from that way - and can only attract other experiences to help them resolve. So, it may well be that there's still so much learning for that person on the other end of that contract. They might contract with you again but of course the quickening is that you've learnt yours quicker and they've got more time to learn theirs, another opportunity, perhaps. But some of them just haven't got it for a few (incarnations). And it's at that point that we don't muck around, and we don't waste time and we get on with it. But at the same time, we fall into a place of compassion with that person a lot quicker because we get it that they're just stuck. And we don't take it personally and we don't waste our time because we know it's just not going to shift with our energy. You know what I mean? We've gotten to that point where we just know we've got to walk on forward with big things that we've contracted with ourselves, not just with them. That's bigger than that contract.

Friend: So, I can keep fast tracking?

Me: Oh, absolutely 100%. Honestly, from what I am getting energetically from him it's totally advised. There's nothing where they're saying, "you should wait until they've caught up". No, there's none of that. That's not helpful. At all. Especially not in your situation.

Friend: Mmm, okay. I'll add a last tangent onto that one. Do you have any visions around fast-tracking that? Any visual images of my work, my family, my living place, really practical visual images.

Me: Well..the 2 big words I've got that he's just said, that I feel that will apply to everything, he said, "NO HIDING".

Friend: Mmm.

Me: That's it. If you hide it doesn't work, not with this situation.

Friend: Wow! Hide my true self, or, hide my being, hide my expression or hide any topic?

Me: Everything. Doesn't work, it's totally disempowering to you to do that. That's what he's showing me.

Friend: I've got like a little – it's not a painful thing right now. I've just realised, the whole time I've had a little, in my right ear a nice little continual reverberation.

Me: Cool, like a little clearing going on yeah? Like tuning into his radio station?

Friend: Like a nice tone, a tone, that's just playing.

Me: Nice.

Friend: Wow! That's just exciting. That's very, very exciting.

Me: Yep it is isn't it?

Friend: If you have time, both of you guys, can you talk more about that manifesting one, manifesting with health manifesting with your physical reality, more about the machinations and keys to that.

Me: So, we are manifesting that which will serve us for our highest good - which might not be what we think it is. And so if we need to manifest something to teach us the next lesson, that will also happen. We can't override it too much because, it's almost like fighting yourself. Because you might have contracted with regards to something to do with your health to help you to learn about something for example that might help you in your career or it might help you in understanding yourself better. So, we can't be too puritanical. We can't be too perfectionistic with our health. We need to be relaxed and allow ourselves to experience what messages are coming through and we're being guided specifically through our connection with our bodies in this universe (on earth). So, this is what we need to do rather than judge it, such as "My health isn't that great - something's wrong. Something's not right." That would be an error. That would be something that we're unnecessarily burdened by so we're getting closer to, "Everything is meant to be, everything that I'm experiencing even my health process that may not seem ideal right now, is perfect and I can certainly tune into whether or not I have contracted this. I can tune into whether or not this is going to lead me somewhere and then that will quicken the recovery. Because if I get what I am meant to do with this, then I will heal from it quicker and I will learn the lessons I am meant to learn quicker and I will meet those people that I'm meant to meet quicker and I will learn how I can perhaps be of better service quicker with going trough this process with healing whatever I'm healing". So, there's all that behind it. So, going in with the intention to manifest perfect health is probably the wrong intention to have because of that. You're almost like saying "If I'm not in perfect health, there's something wrong".

(As I proof read this I have a revelation of what Louise Hay's life would have been like if she'd not had her uncurable cervical cancer in the first place. She would not have discovered how to heal herself naturally through positive thinking and resolving her resentment towards her childhood abuse and rape that she discovered had contributed to its onset. She would not have been able to pass on that knowledge to others through her best seller "You can Heal Your Life" which has sold over 35 million copies worldwide (by 2008) and helped millions harness this knowledge. What would the world be like without the realisations behind her own ability to heal her body from emotional and physical trauma?).

Friend: Yep, yep. Well what about the same principles for trying to manifest those movements in my physical life, with my children in terms of living.

Me: Yes, exactly, he's saying exactly the same thing. He's nodding and he's saying the same thing. He's saying, "That is correct. Instead of judging it, "It's wrong what's happening now" or something like that, it would be, "What am I being nudged in the direction of what I've got to do, so that I learn that quickly, so then things move". So, he's showing me that it's a daily process and it's not something where you have a quick answer, it's something that you feel into. And you go, "Okay, is there something I haven't learnt? Is there a contract I haven't addressed? Is something that is a barrier right now, any barrier?" And if you look at it from those points of view, the moving pace quickens. Rather than thinking it should be here when it's only here. That actually slows the pace down, because you are putting a judgement on it.

Friend: Mmm, yep, yep, okay. I like that. That's cool. Anything else coming through?

Me: No I think that's enough and he's just saying, he's looking forward to talking to you one on one. And I'm actually looking forward to hearing what happens when you have that conversation.

Friend: Oh yeah!

Me: I'm just excited for you honestly. To be honest I'm just excited for you. Like yay! Like hello!

Friend: Yeah! I've been put into this family here, which is perfect with my learning but I'm so excited to connect more to my actual soul family.

Me: Yep and you know what he said to Tony? Tony could talk to him as well. So, there's 2 of you. So that's cool! I'm like, "Oh wow that's great! There's a couple of people that I kind of feel this is my family you know?" I get what you're saying. Because Tony felt comfortable talking to him too.

Friend: Wow, could Tony see or hear him as well? How was he perceiving it?

Me: We were having a conversation where Tony was asking a question and I was answering via Ralph. More than by me hearing Ralph and almost like channelling, it was more like him speaking but at the same time. He felt quite comfortable and was happy to give it a go and connect with Ralph. So, I'm yet to hear back about that yet, but that was just the day before yesterday and yesterday we were really busy. So, you know, timing is everything.

Friend: Wow, wow! Thank you Ralph! Thank you Shell!

Me: You're welcome. He likes to give big hugs, like you know, big warm gooey, kind of intergalactic hugs. So, I don't know if you want to take a moment to let him in.

Friend: Yeah, I read that, that sounds beautiful.

Me: I know it's awesome,

Friend: I had someone else explain like that big pink beautiful energy.

Me: Mmm.

Friend takes a moment to receive an intergalactic hug from Ralph.

Friend: Wow, I can feel like a soft breathing in my right ear when that is happening.

Me: Mmm, I think you told me that there was a sound of breathing in your ear, once from memory.

Friend: Yeah, absolutely.

Me: Maybe was him?

Friend: Yes same place, same sound.

Me: Uhuh.

Friend: It's still there now.

Me: Uhuh. Well I hope you feel as good as I do, haha!

Friend: Hahaha, I sure do birthday girl that was so cool!

Me: Mmm.

Friend: The only one I didn't get. I understand with the 'no hiding' right? Don't hide my soul, my spirit, my expression, but does that include me just like not ringing back and just staying out of touch. Is that hiding or is that healthy?

Me: No, there is just no bones about it, you don't have to hide anything. You don't have to hide how you feel, you don't have to hide why you're not calling back. You don't have to hide anything.

Friend: Yeah. I just got a little worried thinking "Hold on, that doesn't mean I have to contact."

Me: No, not at all, no, no, no! On the contrary. Hiding means you're calling someone because they have an expectation and you're rising to meet their expectation and you're hiding your true feelings. No, the hiding, not hiding, I was seeing flashes of everything and I was just getting wow, like just, no hiding anywhere. Hahaha!

Friend: Yep, I love it. Yeah, I jotted it all down there that was so cool.

Me: Cool.

CHAPTER 8

Questions Found

On 25 April, 2018 I finally transcribed the voice recording I had found – I realised I had sms'd it to myself from Tony's phone. A few questions had already been answered. These are the questions that Tony and I had asked directly following my first conversation with Ralph on 14 April 2018.

Me: Okay some of the questions could be…

Tony: Are they aware of any other people from our universe that have visited before? Do they know anything about our universe?

Me: Do people have to go there to die for their last incarnation?

Tony: When do they know if when we die our soul awakens in other universes, do they know if we die our soul just goes to the spirit place from here? In their universe is there any such thing as a physical body? Do they know anything about the spirit world or is the spirit world merely just another universe?

Me: Any other questions?

Tony: More will come honey.

Me: Is it necessary to visit their universe to understand their process? Or is it just information that some of us can bring back and then once that information is received, it's not necessary to go there? Or they then once they have that information they have to go there to experience it for themselves?

Tony: Do they know who created the portals and are the portals whatever you want to call them, are they specifically designed to enable other universes to evolve? Is that their purpose?

Me: Is the purpose of their last incarnation universe to share that with all other universes? And that other question you had – are other universes the same – are they different?

Toy: Is it safe to use the portal to travel to other universes. Is it dangerous to use the portal to go to unknown universes?

Me: How do you (Ralph) resolve your past life stuff through the processes that you can see. How does it resolve, how does it heal? Is it merely through conversation or are there other healings that need to happen, or processes that need to happen between 2 people? Or are there people in their universe helping other people like we do to resolve these things? Or is it merely through the interactions that they are having between each other, the contracts. How do the contracts work that people have? Do they communicate with people on the other side?

Tony: That have passed.

Me: Yeah and if they do, what does that look like?

Tony: Yeah that's what I asked earlier on when people pass are they doing to another dimension or the spirit world which is not another universe.

Me: I feel like this is a prophecy – not just information.

Tony: Mmm.

CHAPTER 9

Answers Found

28 April 2018 – Conversation 7

This morning I felt like experimenting trying to record my conversation real time by typing directly into my computer whilst talking to Ralph. I've copied and pasted the questions that Tony and I had initially thought of, to see if we've covered all those questions.

Tony: Are they aware of any other people from our universe that have visited before? Do they know anything about our universe?

Ralph: Yes, we are aware of people from your universe who have visited before. I also have companions here who talk to me about their travel and interactions. Many of your species of humanity in your current form have visited and are learning what you are learning now. There is a collective. It would be nice to see you get together and unify your learnings. We know a vast amount about your universe as we have lived through many incarnations at every stage of your universe – in our own. So, there is a vast amount of information at each stage that we can impart to you.

You asked whilst you were walking, the other day, through the bush walk whether we come to your universe and embody rocks, trees etc. Yes, we do. Why do we do it? Because sometimes, we have contracted to communicate to humans via nature. And the only way that they will feel us, is if we take presence there. So, we can embody individually or collectively the same vibrational frequency in an area. This does raise the frequency of the location as well. For instance, Sedona. But in its simplest form, it can be that we have a connection with a tree, rock, crystal, even thorough an animal, that is more like a guardianship contract and it gives us the ability to do that, in a more tangible form for you. At this stage of our evolution, some of us are very ready to resolve, yet we have multiverse contracts to fulfil. It is not the same as walk-ins where we take over a host. It is more of a direct contract to make contact with the person who we have contracted with.

Me: Do people have to go there to die for their last incarnation?

Ralph: We covered this question before, so you know that the answer to this one is no. Not everyone on their last incarnation has to come here to be resolved. However, in addition to what I just said, we can contract to be present until the final incarnation consciousness stage. Such as I have. I knew that this is what I would do. As do you Michelle. Remember how you felt when you heard a person say that they wanted to go home to the planet they came from and not come back to help humanity. It was like a dagger to your heart. That was indicative that you are charted to indeed return. You have committed to the service of humanity. What other species of humans (who think they are above humanity) don't realise is that they too are just human. Even if they feel a little strange here – alien if you like – in this world, your world, in this incarnation, they fail to realise that they are another extension of humanity's consciousness. Remember how you felt when a relative couldn't accept reincarnation, especially of an existing family member who had passed who was now returning to the family in another form? That rejection of that concept, was like a huge stone wall they had placed in front of you in connecting with them on a deeper level. This too is indicative of how strongly this is your truth. You cannot deny your truth, even if others strongly oppose your view. Otherwise, you will suffer so much internally, that it will feel like it is crushing you.

Me: Okay thanks Ralph, this makes perfect sense. We will move onto the next question now.

Tony: Do they know if when we die our soul awakens in other universes, do they know if we die our soul just goes to the spirit place from here? In their universe is there any such thing as a physical body? Do they know anything about the spirit world or is the spirit world merely just another universe?

Ralph: Souls from your universe are not reincarnated into our universe. The only exception is when one has breached their own universe via being walk-in into another universe. We've covered this question. The only other exception is if (such as my situation) I have contracted to assist those at this final stage and created karmic ties with other individuals. However, I do not have to be available at the final stage of another's incarnation in a bodiless form, in your universe, if I am resolved and they are not. As you know, there are no physical bodies in our universe at this stage. The physical would not survive at this vibrational frequency of consciousness. We know of the spirit world as I have described it to you. We do have contact with those who are not ready to incarnate into their final incarnation. So, this process may seem confusing to you. However, there are those that are in spirit form that can be a bit confused about where to go to next to do their final stage of planning – the respite before the final incarnation – where they would meet the high council. However, you have done much work in this area where you have assisted others to pass over to the light, especially lightworkers that remained behind the help others, such as in 9/11 at ground zero.

Me: Yes, I spent many months back in 2009 visiting different sites (astrally) that I was called to visit to help lightworkers move on.

Ralph: Yes, so you are well versed in this. We also are well versed in this at this final stage. Well some of us are interested – who have a calling to do so. As you know, there are people here who may be in deep depression. This blocks their gifts to do this level of mediumship. And also, it is introspective, so they have no interest in being of service at this level.

Me: Great, that gives me clarity. Now back to the next questions on our list.

Me: Is it necessary to visit their universe to understand their process? Or is it just information that some of us can bring back and then once that information is received, it's not necessary to go there? Or they then once they have that information they have to go there to experience it for themselves?

Ralph: No, it's not necessary to visit our universe to understand this process as you now know. This knowledge is destined to be learned and passed on to humanity, just as you are doing now. Many who hear it will 'just know' it is true. Other's will fight it as they feel fear of the truth – that everyone will know everything about them. This is a shame-based response. They don't want to be seen. They don't want their imperfection – their perceived imperfections – to be seen. That is scary. That is the sole reason they fight it. Anyone who feels called to visit can do so. But it is not necessary. And we urge you not to come here if you are scared of the concept. Only come with the intention of peace, otherwise you create karmic ties here with us and potentially delay the final incarnation 'resolving' of some people.

Tony: Do they know who created the portals and are the portals whatever you want to call them, are they specifically designed to enable other universes to evolve? Is that their purpose?

Ralph: The All created the intergalactic portals, you call worm holes, for the purpose of evolving humanities consciousness in the spirit of unity. Although our universes are separate, we share commonalities and we are destined to help each other.

Me: Is the purpose of their last incarnation universe to share that with all other universes? And that other question you had – are other universes the same – are they different?

Ralph: The purpose of our last incarnation universe is to resolve. Only some of us have contracted to share this information with your current universe's consciousness. And also, we continue to do that with some people in future stages of your humanity's universe. All universes are similar, the same in evolving consciousness but with some differences in the finer details. The grander scale is that humanity's purpose is set to evolve and that is the commonality shared between universes.

Toy: Is it safe to use the portal to travel to other universes. Is it dangerous to use the portal to go to unknown universes?

Ralph: If you astral travel with the intention of peace, it is safe. If you tried to physically travel to this universe that is now bodiless, it would be unsafe – you would disintegrate. If you travel to our universe with an energy of fear, you may find that all you see here is fear, a mere reflection of your own internal reality.

Me: How do you (Ralph) resolve your past life stuff through the processes that you can see. How does it resolve, how does it heal? Is it merely through conversation or there other healings that need to happen, or processes that need to happen between 2 people or are there people in their universe helping other people like we do to resolve these things? Or is it merely through the interactions that they are having between each other, the contracts. How do the contracts work that people have? Do they communicate with people on the other side.

Ralph: Past lives are resolved when, during a conversation the giver of their reality is sharing with another. The receiver sees and validates all that the giver is sharing because they can see what has led them to that point. They mention this, what they see. But it goes deeper than that. They have an incredible empathic understanding. Looking at the person, as it were, as if it was them. They feel compassion for this person. This person represents how they feel about themselves. If they feel pity, the receiver is not resolved. If they feel empathy and understanding and love, they are resolved and they give this energy to the person sharing. They emit it from their vibrational frequency. The person sharing either receives it and also feels that for themselves or they can reject it and choose to 'not resolve' that particular issue at that time. They may require more time to re-experience and share with others before they are ready and at a place of self-forgiveness, self-love. Also, the other element at play here is, the person sharing being able to accept the other person who is listening to them. Perhaps the receiver has shared some of their experience and this has been judged by the giver. They are then not resolved with the mirror, the reflection, that the receiver is also reflecting back to the giver. So there are 2 levels. As I mentioned to you previously, this can be done in groups. Group work is very popular here. Now this might sound relatively simple. An exchange. But, it is also very powerful. How one feels about themselves and others is everything here. It's the feelings that are paramount. The contracts of previous lives play a big part. Often in the sharing, that is how the contracts are uncovered, understood and resolved. And yes, we communicate with people on the other side (that have passed) as I previously mentioned. Well some of us. And not from your universe. They don't hang here. They are tied to your universe karmically. So only those from our universe who have previously passed, are here. That is one big difference between our bodiless form here too. If we are in the middle world on passing but not having gone to the light as yet, we cannot transverse universes. We don't have the freedom to do that. No one does.

CHAPTER 10

Enough for Now

3 May 2018: Conversation 8

Me: Okay, so I know it's been a few days since our last conversation. However, I have been very aware of your presence. On 29 April 2018 I was at the Discovery Expo festival filming and had a wonderful Spiritual Guide Artist by the name of Sarah, channel through the energy that I felt coming in from you above (that is now the cover of this book). During that time, I felt very impacted by the energy and was shaking internally from my solar plexus to my feet. I felt like the higher vibrational energy and information you had brought me over the past couple of weeks was being integrated into my whole body, on a whole new level. To get a visual of the energy was huge for me, as all I see was the blackness of nothing and some moving energy. But I feel she captured how that energy looked even more and to see it with physical sight, made it even more real. I realised the power of using the arts to channel through these high vibe frequencies, really amplifies them on the physical plane.

Ralph: Yes it certainly does and rightly so, as you are in physical form. Today when you were speaking with Tony about whether he had followed up checking in with me, and he responded that he had but not received information in the form that you had, this is a perfect example of educating others that how we receive information and energy is different for different people and at different times too. You were receiving the energy of our conversations in a whole different form when Sarah was channelling through the energy. It was you – not a spiritual guide in physical form that she was drawing. It was you the physical being you could 'see' on the artwork. It was the galactic energy that she drew above the diamond that was representative of what our consciousness brings (from my universe). There was a meeting of energies in the middle of the diamond. It was also channelling and streaming through into you. It was no mistake you had just witnessed a diamond activation by Raghida at the festival an hour before your channelled artwork. It all came together in perfect synchronicity to affirm and validate your experience. It is no mistake that the people who connected with you at the festival came to you. It was no mistake the people who did not, did not. You are correct in saying that the people who do not hang around you – nay are repelled by you – are to be congratulated. They are living their own vibration and being authentic to that. That is not a criticism of you, nor is it a condemnation of themselves. They are honouring the precise and perfect measure of vibration they need to be activated in their own consciousness. It's not always about how you do it, what you have to offer others, that makes it valid. It is about them, their needs, their required learning and their unique journey. Once we all get this, we will no longer take anything personally.

Me: Yes, and I feel a little shaky right now. It is permeating more through me now as I am writing this (typing this) directly from our conversation. Also, I have been feeling small heat areas on my body. Like a warm hand is pressing on me or grabbing me. Is that you? It's like a localised hot spot on different parts of my body. Then it goes away. It happened a few times over the past few days.

Ralph: You are becoming even more sensitive. Remember the warm hug I gave you after the first couple of conversations? It was like an 'all body warmth'. Yes, that is me, making myself known to you. That you are now able to physically feel that warmth, even when we are not in conversation. I am still communicating with you.

Me: Do particular areas mean something? I remember once was on my right forearm and just now I felt it on my left hip. Just a little warm spot. I've never ever felt that before so randomly.

Ralph: I'm glad you asked! I don't like to nag. But sometimes humanity requires repetition before they notice and as you have been very focused and preoccupied with filming and work over the past few days, I was reaching out to communicate with you in other ways. By the way, your focus has been spiritualised, I wasn't trying to interfere with that.

Me: Ah, okay, I get it! And it totally fits in with what we are talking about right now, which is that Spirit connects with us in different ways. It validates that. To get our attention. I still don't know what it means though and would appreciate clarification, if there's a specific message related.

Ralph: You also had 2 pain areas right? Once on right temple and it went away, then on left. That was last night.

Me: Correct! Weird sharp pains and then they totally went away. I never ever get that. It's like these are pains or warm sensations that are odd. Never before experienced, or anything like it. Except a few times I've had the warm sensations on my arm. Not on my hip or localised warmth on parts of my body though.

Ralph: Okay, allow me to explain. The warm parts on your arm are me trying to get your attention, a bit like a tap on your shoulder. If this happens, just stop, take a moment and we can have a chat. I have important information. It will get through some other way, through something someone else does or says, but I am offering you a short cut. And I know how much you love a good short cut.

Me: Okay! That makes sense. And also, the fact that this was the only feeling that I'd had repeat, it helps me realise, you were reaching out to give me a short cut. Sweet!

Ralph: The hip today, was to trigger your memory of a conversation you had with Jean Sheehan recently when you were interviewing her for High Vibe Hunter TV and you pulled one of her medical intuition cards and you got the pelvis card, remember?

Me: Of course! And it was all about assimilation. And we are talking about assimilation of energy. I also got the skin card as well which is about absorbing. Absorption and assimilation. It couldn't be more relevant or validating for the very conversation we are having. Wow! It makes sense and is somewhat prophetic as to what was about to happen. Even though we filmed the episode a couple of months ago, we only published the episode the week that you and I first consciously connected. Bingo!

Ralph: Okay, you've got the message loud and clear. Well done.

Me: Sure have, phew! I understand that the information is one thing, absorbing it. Then actually assimilating it and integrating it into my whole body is another. And that coincides with a lot of what Tony has been going through as well. Makes so much sense.

Ralph: Shall we move to the temple area now?

Me: Yes, the pain in my temples. Albeit brief, I was wondering, what the hell was going on.

Ralph: There is another load of information about to come through. This is a warning. In a good way. It will be balanced. It will come through the right brain and then go through to the left.

Me: So I'm being prepared?

Ralph: Yes, that's why I wanted to speak to you today. I know we've so far covered validating your sensation experiences. That's really great. But that's not the actual huge download you are being prepared for.

Me: Oh, okay! I'm feeling wobbly in my tummy and a sprinkle of energetic madness at the base of my spine.

Ralph: Understandable that you are nervous. It's a compliment to the energy about to stream through.

Me: I understand you are preparing me. I am excited. I will just take a quick break and return.

Ralph: Okay, I will be waiting.

I had a quick loo and water break and felt refreshed and really anticipated the next instalment of my conversation with Ralph.

Me: Okay, I'm ready, not at all sure of what you are going to tell me, but completely open.

Ralph: This one is really important. Not a lot of people will get it, but it must be communicated to you.

Me: Okay, I'm listening.

Ralph: This is about why we become guides. How this exists. What motivates us. How it all works for us in our humanity. How it is different from Ascended Masters, or the Angelic realm.

Me: As you were talking I just got a localised hot spot at the front of my left ear.

Ralph: Well, I did say it would go in through your right brain which relates to your left side.

Me: That makes sense, I'm listening to this new information.

Ralph: Yes, hot spots, when they are not from a toxic injection of energy, are actually very helpful in ascertaining messages being communicated.

Me: Makes sense. Go on about this new information.

Ralph: Well, it's more important than you realise to become a guide whilst still in human form (well not physically) in my world. We can only do so much in our realm. We may have run out of contracts between those in our realm and have only got contracts outside of our realm. This is best explained in this way. Standard contracts and universal contracts. Standard contracts are created within the same universe. Universal contacts are created to serve the greater evolving consciousness of humanity. They are necessary and go beyond 'personal growth' or 'resolving'. Universal contracts are diverse. They are not simply explained. However, we have covered some of the more common forms that we can take to fulfil these contracts. For instance, we can take form in inanimate objects – you can feel us when you hold something. Like a rock, crystal or even a piece of jewellery. You can feel us as a presence. You can sense us in nature. But the less obvious form we take, is in the shadows of your consciousness. We may guide you, as I did you for several years, but you didn't know it was me. I only had your best intentions at heart and of course you knew that. You had distinguished how to tell the difference between lower or higher guidance thanks to Archangel Michael. However, it is only when we WANT to show ourselves, do we show ourselves. And I mean this in whatever form. It can be as you 'hear' me. Or as you 'feel' me. Or as in your friend's case, she hears my breath. It can be that your husband is able to get a greater sense of 'peace' and 'relaxation' when he concentrates on my energy. Then later, this filters down into his conscious mind through is claircogniscene or 'aha' moments. We are here for a reason. This is not for self-gain at all. We are here (in your universe) for the greater evolution of consciousness. Most of us are completely resolved, yet we must remain in the realm of bodiless form and maintain a sense of peace, to help others continue to resolve, in part, but also to be of service to the greater expanses of the universe. For instance, we may not have any more karmic ties to resolve with another in our bodiless universe, we may be completely resolved, but we have contracts to fulfil on a grander scale with helping others to resolve. And also, as in the instance with us, to help you communicate this important information. You have been well placed and well positioned right now with all the people and communication streams you need to continue to get the messages that I have communicated to you out there into the greater conscious awareness stream.

Me: I see, this means a great deal. You are doing everything you are doing from a place of freedom. Free will still exists.

Ralph: Yes indeed. And also from a place of...

At that moment, I couldn't continue to type. A great wave of warmth hit me. It enveloped my whole body. I completely couldn't think at all. It was the most peaceful feeling. I really 'got' what it felt like to be that at peace. To be in that much freedom that it also connects us to others. I don't know what Ralph was going to say next, but I felt it. Perhaps he felt understood and perhaps all the barriers to his reality and my reality were broken down. Was I experiencing his reality?

Me: I lost it! Well, I lost hearing you! I was overtaken by a huge warm blanket of peace that totally wiped my mind.

Ralph: I told you, you would take it in through the right brain.

Me: Wow, I feel that pain, right now.

Ralph: Yes, it's a feeling. It's not inside the box. It's an experience completely outside the box. One cannot explain it. One must experience it to understand.

Me: I understood it to a point, and then wham! It hit me.

Ralph: On some level, this means something more to me than anything ever has. It's hard to describe. What you experienced, was a feeling of overwhelming gratitude of me being understood. We don't seek to be understood. We are beyond that. But on some level, being understood still has impact. Still has validation. I feel that welled up inside me. I wanted to communicate more, but I too lost my words.

Me: This is amazing. I know it must be so hard to describe, but I can't undo the fact I now understand you. And also now I understand how it feels to be understood!

Ralph: We spend so many endless hours helping without the attachment or expectation to be understood. But it is a fundamental need. And it does not go unnoticed or unfelt, just because we do not have the expectation.

Me: No, of course not. You still feel, that's endless, right?

Ralph: Yes, that is what makes us human. That, and consciousness of ourselves as singular and interconnected beings.

Me: I'm dying to hear what you were going to say next though. Can you attempt to describe it for me in words?

Ralph: Well, free will still exists. We are also aware of our contracts, remember I told you that? Well, when you hear contracts, you perhaps view that like a 'legally binding contract'. It is not so. These contracts – the universal ones – are the greatest gift to us than you could imagine. Remember I told you how we feel every time we see someone resolve an issue? It's such a joyful feeling. Well, being a catalyst for that, on a grander scale, feels even more amazing. To know that we can be the catalyst for so many of you being activated and to save you from the endless pit of depression of unresolved business, is an incredible feeling. We know that our contracts – at this level – serve a purpose way beyond ourselves. We know that these contracts also assist our world to resolve as well as I mentioned before, some of our crew here depart to live in your world for a time. And they create karmic ties and they create a prolonged experience. As we serve your world with these universal contracts, they then serve our world.

Me: I am seeing that the last incarnation of all universes finally catch up with each other.

(It was a vision that made so much sense. I saw that the very last incarnation of the very last souls were all in bodiless form and that each universe at that point, were helping each other get across the line to 'resolving'. The very point of unity consciousness. Multiversal consciousness! No one gets left out ever).

Ralph: You see correctly.

Me: Wow! That's mammoth. A lot to take in.

Ralph: Hence the head ache?

Me: Great sense of humour Ralph. Good one.

Ralph: You felt it again during that last bit.

Me: Yes, is that the last bit of information for now?

Ralph: Yes, for now. Go chill out.

Me: I will, thank you again. And I mean it, thank you.

Ralph: Thanks for your understanding. A first for me.

I went and had some lunch and a good break. I didn't allow myself to 'think' about it and just chilled out and watched some TV as I ate some warming soup and relaxed. I knew though, that it wasn't the end of the messages for today. I read over all that I had channelled and it was really BIG. I felt like something had happened that doesn't happen very often in this universe. Ah, that pain again now as I type. I'm going in.

Me: Hey I'm back.

Ralph: Back for more conscious torture!

Me: Very funny. I do know that the only way to rid myself of this occasional sharp pain is to allow the information to come through. I'm really getting this connection now.

Ralph: It is important information today. The body doesn't want to hold it back, all in one place, it wants to disperse it through your body.

Me: I just can't imagine what could be more important than what you just shared with me. Really, what could it be?

Ralph: Well, just wanting to thank you so much for understanding the bigger picture of why we choose to be guides. And I want to expand on why we are different from Ascended Masters and Angelic beings. It needs to be clarified.

Me: Ah! That big...

Ralph: Yes, that big. Some people think that Ascended Masters or the Angelic Realm have been incarnated human beings. However, it is the other way round. They have been Ascended Masters and Angelic Beings and then have chosen to have a human experience. However, their concentrated archetypal energy exists before and beyond the human physical form. They are striving to educate in one concentrated stream of consciousness. That is their purpose. They are very focused. We are focusing on the integration of all these streams of energy. The energy that they bring exists within us all as an individual and collective species within one and across the multiverse. So we are the labrynth. We are all the labrynth. We seek to assist this interconnectedness to become actualised and conscious. It already exists, yet it is the job of each human to become conscious of all the interconnectedness with these concentrated higher vibrational frequencies.

Me: Wow, that's different! I understand it though. It makes a lot of sense. And that you mentioned that in the example of Jesus that each universe has that Christ consciousness incarnate, so that's a good example then? We all have to have that Christ experience to connect to that consciousness?

Ralph: Yes, exactly. So these higher vibrational beings are always in existence in each moment. Right now, you have a plethora of these vibrations at your feet, at your disposal. They never, ever go away.

Me: It's like I'm a kid in a candy store, but haven't turned the light on to every section of the shop?

Ralph: Well, you have, but many others haven't.

Me: We can choose to access any and all higher vibrational frequencies at any given moment, it's up to us?

Ralph: You turn the light on.

Me: We flick the switch, but it was already there.

Ralph: Exactly.

Me: And the Angelic realm works in the same way?

Ralph: Yes, they serve different functions that are specific. You know about these, you've already written about them.

Me: Yes, I remember in 'Making Light Work' my first book, I tunned into their specific jobs.

Ralph: And you know that you cannot unlearn what you've learned, however as a human being, you cannot consciously access it all at any given moment. But you can access what you need. In order to access what you need, you need to know what it is you are lacking.

Me: Hence the darkness, the shadow, is required to open us to the light.

Ralph: Exactly.

Me: I get it. So, our job as humans is to firstly recognise what we need, secondly want to access it (free will) and thirdly access it. And the final step is to integrate it all.

Ralph: Exactly.

Me: So the difference between me and you is that we are not really any different at all. You are more aware of course of what you have integrated and what is yet to be integrated, but we are both the same in what our purpose is, what humanity's purpose is.

Ralph: Yes, and we are not that different when it all boils down to it. Yes, we may have life purposes that appear different from lifetime to lifetime, but they all serve the greater purpose. Humanity doesn't realise it, but it is serving the greater purpose of humanity ALL THE TIME – whether it knows it or not.

Me: Yes, because before things are integrated, they are unconscious. So, when someone is behaving unconscious towards us, our learning is how we reconcile that part of ourselves and we are at peace with that.

Ralph: Hence why shadow work is so important in the integration of humanity.

Me: Both the dark and light aspects matter. We need to access and integrate the light and we also need to understand and integrate the shadow.

Ralph: And if you only do one, you become out of balance. If you only integrated the darker aspects of your nature without help from the higher vibrations, there would not be proper integration. There may be inquisitive investigation of the shadow, but there you could get led astray, as is the nature of lower vibrational frequencies to keep us distracted.

Me: And if we only focused on integrating the lighter aspects of all the higher frequencies, but feared our shadow or unconscious bits, we would be living a cover up, a lie.

Ralph: We would merely be hiding some of ourselves in shame.

Me: Now I don't have the pain, but just felt like the corner of my right forehead was bulging out. What was that??

Ralph: Your mind is expanding literally. And this is reflecting back in your right hemisphere.

Me: Far out.

Ralph: I know, the physical body is pretty amazing.

Me: Now I feel that it has moved, I feel the corner of my right eyebrow – to eye near my nose and middle of my forehead is really activated. And my right ear lobe is throbbing slightly.

Ralph: There are many activations at play. Just enjoy it.

Me: Okay, so it's all part of the same thing?

Ralph: Most definitely – it's clearing all your chakras – third eye, ear, now your throat.

Me: Yep, I feel that. Like a huge lump in my throat! Wowza.

I stop for a second to take a drink of water and catch my breath.

Me: I feel that this is enough information for a book. Do I need to write anymore?

Ralph: There is more to tell you, you have some conversations with others to record. But apart from that. I think the world has enough information to absorb and assimilate. Don't you?

Me: Yes, I do. I wasn't sure how long the book would be, but I feel it's definitely enough for most to read and take in. You're right.

Printed in the United States
By Bookmasters